KIDDING AROUND

PARIS

A YOUNG PERSON'S GUIDE TO THE CITY

REBECCA CLAY

ILLUSTRATED BY MARY LAMBERT

John Muir Publications
Santa Fe, New Mexico

Special thanks to Best Western International, Inc., for providing accommodations for the author in Paris while she researched this book. For information on Best Western Hotels, call 800-528-1234.

John Muir Publications, P.O. Box 613, Santa Fe, NM 87504

First edition. First printing

Clay, Rebecca, 1956-
    Kidding around Paris: a young person's guide to the city/ Rebecca Clay: illustrated by Mary Lambert.—1st ed.
        p. cm.
    Summary: A guide designed to introduce young people to French culture as well as to the sights of Paris.
    ISBN 0-945465-82-3
    1. Paris (France)—Description—1975-
—Guide-books—Juvenile literature. 2. Children—
Travel—France—Paris—Juvenile literature. [1. Paris
(France)—Description—Guides.]   I. Lambert, Mary, ill.
II. Title.
DC708.C56   1991
914.4'36104839—dc20   91-8506
                                                          CIP
                                                          AC

For Zdzislaw, Claude, the Santistèbes and Myers and tous les enfants de Paris et de l'Amérique.

Distributed to the book trade by:
W.W. Norton & Company, Inc.
New York, New York

Typeface: Trump Mediaeval
Designer: Joanna V. Hill
Typesetter: Copygraphics, Santa Fe, New Mexico
Printer: Guynes Printing Company of New Mexico

Contents

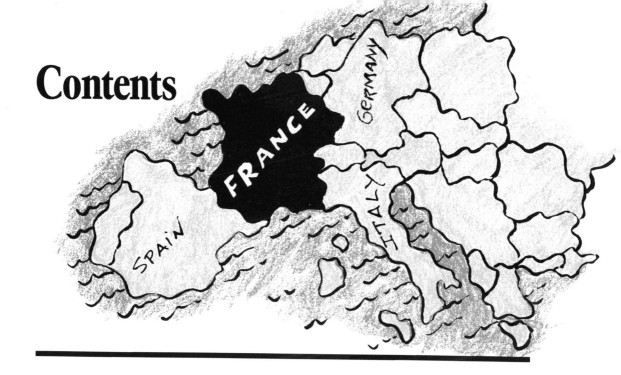

1. City of Light

By the 1400s, Paris was still pitch black at night. The entire city was lit by only three lanterns. But by 1829, it was the first city in the world to glow with gas lamps. That's one reason they call Paris the City of Light!

The city of Paris is a feast for the senses. Take a look at the graceful, lyrical lines of its buildings and monuments and parks. Hear the musical rhythm of the French language, whether spoken by short-tempered waiters, long-winded politicians, or everyone in-between. And smell the aroma of Parisian cuisine, from the sizzling sugar of crepes being flipped on a street corner to the salty warmth of French fries (the real thing) on a café plate.

Paris is many things to many people. To some, it's pure romance. To others, it's all history. And to still others, it's a perfect mix of both.

Turn a corner and you'll see the mark of a Parisian, an invader, or a visitor, maybe made ten years ago, a hundred years ago, or more than a thousand. From the crumbling ruins of Roman baths, built around the time of Jesus, to the shiny Géode of the City of Science and Industry, built in 1986, Paris offers the sights and sounds of a powerful past and present.

Paris is sometimes called the City of Light, and for centuries, it has been considered one of the most famous and most beautiful cities in the world. Today, it's the capital of France, where politicians, bankers, and artists live and work side by side.

Plus, you'll find just about every nationality in Paris, from the people who left France's former colonies in Africa and Asia to those who left the old repressive governments of the Soviet Union and Eastern Europe. Paris has long been the land of immigrants, too, because it often welcomes people in need of sanctuary and a home. And this has created separate neighborhoods, including Chinese, Jewish, Arab, African, Parisian, and even American.

Paris grew from a tiny settlement clustered around the islands in the Seine to a fast-paced city of millions of people. It's divided into twenty arrondissements, or sections, each with its own town hall and unique character. You'll probably spend most of your time along the Seine, in the 1st, 2nd, 3rd, 4th, 5th, 6th, 7th, and 8th arrondissements.

Getting around Paris is not tricky as long as you remember a few basic rules. First of all, most street names change at each intersection, which can be confusing. Wherever you go, bring a good map that lists street names and their exact location. It's easy to get lost, and you might not find an English-speaking person to help you right away.

The subway, called the Métro, has been running since 1900. The system can take you just about anywhere you want to go, and you shouldn't have to wait more than a few minutes for a train. But be prepared for a crowd: at least four million people ride the subway trains every day.

Each of the city's fifteen subway lines is known by its destination, so you need to look at the subway map for your stop and then trace the line to its end. For example, if you want to get off at Georges V, you must take the train that heads for Pont de Neuilly or Château de Vincennes,

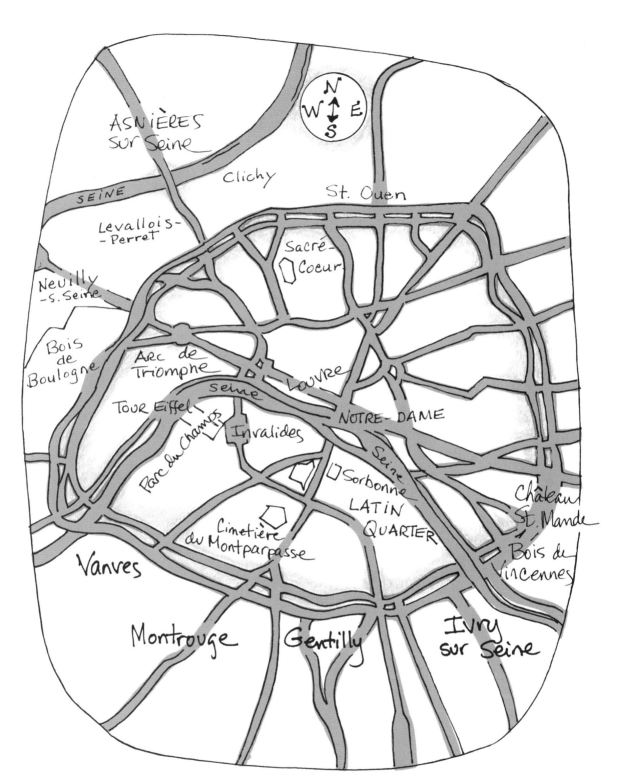

depending on whether you are heading west or east. Many stops have more than one line serving them. Keep an eye out for the singers and musicians who often entertain subway riders. Many of them are American!

Métro and bus tickets cost about 5 francs a piece, but you can buy them in packs of ten for less or pick up a pass for a reduced fare. If you'll be doing a lot of museums, save money by also picking up a discount museum pass from a cashier in the Métro. Just ask!

Buses can seem complicated, but they're a great way to see the city as you slowly pass through the different neighborhoods. Bus stops are marked with a round orange and yellow sign with the bus numbers on it. Just under the sign is a chart of the bus's zigzag route. Pick up a *Guide Général de Paris* in any bookstore for a detailed guide to the Métro, bus, and neighborhoods. But the very best way to see Paris is on foot.

Wherever you go in the world and you mention Paris, often the first thing people will do is lick their lips, simply because French food is some of the very best in the world. So don't always head for one of the American fast food chains or American-style restaurants that are opening up all over the city. The French know how to cook!

If you're absolutely dying for something American, try the spare ribs at Chicago Meat Packers near the Forum des Halles or the clam chowder at Lunch Time near the Place de la Concorde. There's also barbecued chicken at Randy & Jay's and Mexican chili con carne at Susan's Place, both in the Latin Quarter. American students love to hang out at Cactus Charly's not far from the Champs-Elysées.

Most small Parisian shops, businesses, and even restaurants close every afternoon for several hours, usually from 2:00 to 4:00 p.m.

Many Parisian museums and tourist attractions are closed one day a week, usually Monday or Tuesday. Be sure to check the back of this book for more info, before it's too late!

Did you know the croissant is actually a French pastry and the word means "crescent"? Perhaps you eat it stuffed with jelly or cheese. The French never do! They always serve their croissants empty.

When you're out touring the city, and you just need a snack, here are a few good choices. In the summer, on many street corners, you'll find a vendor who is pouring crepe batter on a round skillet, filling it with butter, sugar, chocolate, or jelly, folding it into a cone, slipping it into a paper holder, and handing it to someone who stuffs it into his or her mouth even before paying for it! That's how delicious crepes are!

Plus, in the summer, you'll always find cafés and little grocery stores with an ice cream freezer out front. You won't find any fancy flavors or get a huge dripping scoop, but you will get a small cone with a delicious ball of chocolate, strawberry, or vanilla or an assortment of sherbets. If you see a sign for *glace* you're in the right place. That word means ice cream!

Come wintertime, when the air is biting cold and the streets are dressed up for Christmas, you'll see vendors roasting and selling snack-size bags of chestnuts, a typical Parisian treat, or other warm nuts. The French like chestnuts in many forms, and mashed potatoes are often replaced with whipped chestnuts on a holiday table.

You might enjoy visiting a Parisian department store, such as Printemps, Galeries Lafayette, Le Bon Marche, or Samaritaine. Check out the free fashion show at Galeries Lafayette every Wednesday morning and at Printemps every Tuesday morning. Plus, around Christmastime, pass by the display windows in front of Printemps for a peek at the animated dolls all dressed up in colorful costumes.

To find out what's happening in Paris, there are a few publications you can pick up at the many newsstands you'll see everywhere. *Passion* is a monthly magazine written in English which lists events for kids and adults. The *Free Voice* is a free monthly newspaper you can pick up at English-language bookstores.

The *Pariscope* comes out on Wednesdays, and although its listings are in French, you should be able to figure out the movie schedule. Remember, the French often use military time in the afternoon and evening, meaning that 2:00 p.m. is usually written 14h, and 8:00 p.m. is written 20h. The *h* stands for *heures* (pronounced urr), hours or o'clock.

One thing you'll notice pretty quickly is that there are very few drinking fountains. If you do find one, you'll be very lucky if it works. The best thing to do before you set out in the morning for your city hike is to buy a bottle of water or juice and carry it in your backpack. Otherwise, you'll either go thirsty or pay a super high price for a glass of juice or soda at a café. So, imagine you're crossing a desert and bring your own H_2O!

At the end of the book, you'll find a brief pronunciation guide to help you use some important survival words.

Keep track of the rate for changing your American dollars into French francs. The rate is usually between five and seven francs for one dollar. You'll also be using ten-franc coins and paper money printed in pink, blue, and yellow.

2. The Tallest Flagpole in the World

Across the river from the Eiffel Tower, in the gardens to the right, you'll find the Trocadero Aquarium. It's in an underground cave and shows off a beautiful assortment of freshwater fish.

What is the one image that always makes you think of Paris? If you thought of the **Eiffel Tower**, you are absolutely right.

It's the first place most visitors go. And for good reason. Even though it looks small now, the Eiffel Tower was the tallest structure in the world for forty-one years, from 1889 until 1930. And the view from the third level is truly awesome.

Before you squeeze into one of the tower's four elevator cars, or start trekking up the 1,652 steps of its winding staircase, here's the history of this giant tangle of pig iron.

First of all, the Eiffel Tower was not made to last into the 1990s. Gustav Eiffel, the genius who designed the tower, never intended for you to lay eyes on it. He had it built for the 1889 Paris Universal Exposition, and it was supposed to be pulled down in 1909 when the huge fair was over. Some Parisians at the time definitely wanted it torn down. They said it was the ugliest thing they had ever seen.

The tower weighs 7,000 tons, and it took three hundred men over two years to put the whole thing together with two and a half million rivets. Talk about an erector set!

The elevator will drop you off at one of three levels. The third is the best. There, at each side of the closed-in platform, you'll have an illuminated picture of the main streets and buildings in all directions. That way you can pick out the areas you recognize, such as La Défense skyscraper area to the west, the Arc de Triomphe and the Sacre-Coeur Basilica toward the north and northeast, Notre-Dame Cathedral to the east, and the Montparnasse Tower to the southeast.

It's usually windy up there and you'll probably have a slight sensation of swaying, but don't worry. With stone foundations that go 40 feet into the ground, Eiffel didn't build his tower to fall over!

Back on the ground, you can relax in the tower's park, called the **Champ-de-Mars**, or visit the museums on the other side of the river. The most interesting are the **Musée de l'Homme** (Museum of Man), with its collection of costumes and materials from cultures around the world, and the **Musée de la Marine** (Maritime Museum), with its collection of real and model ships.

Many American children also live in Paris. They usually attend American bilingual or regular French schools. Their parents often work for the U.S. government or corporations or they may be artists.

This is also the place where the skateboarders and roller skaters in town find their biggest challenges. Watch the Parisian hotshots make some death-defying moves on wheels. They might teach you (or you might teach them) a few new tricks!

If you'd rather read, head for the **American Library** on the rue du General Camou, a few blocks over from the Eiffel Tower and the Champ-de-Mars. Not a bad selection of juvenile and adult books in English, considering this is a French city. You have to be a member to borrow a book, but you're welcome to hang out and see what they have (they do charge a small fee for admission).

The library is located in a typical Parisian neighborhood. School gets out around 4:30 and you may see children heading home for a snack, or *goûter*. They might have a baguette under their arm, too, on which they're going to spread a creamy chocolate or nugget paste. Look at what many of them are wearing on their backs. It looks like a briefcase and is called a *cartable*.

If it's a nice day, you'll often see the French shutters and windows flung open on the first-floor apartments. That's where the concierge lives. She's usually Portuguese and keeps a sharp eye on who enters and leaves her building. If you were a Parisian child in her building, she would make sure you didn't play in the hallway or make too much noise!

3. Paris Inside Out

The second most popular attraction for American visitors is the **Centre Pompidou**, which was built between 1972 and 1977. Like the Eiffel Tower, it's made out of steel. But the center is actually a library and a museum that shows off a good collection of modern art.

It sure doesn't look like a museum. The center was named after the man who was president of France in the late 1960s and early 1970s, Georges Pompidou. He wanted to create an ultra-modern multipurpose cultural center within the ancient neighborhood that surrounds it.

One British and one Italian architect got together and designed a building with its insides out. The idea shocked a lot of people at first. The brightly colored tubes and funnels that criss-cross and stick out on the outside carry all the utilities, such as water, gas, and air, that most buildings pack inside their walls. A glassed-in escalator snakes up along the front of the center.

But before you go in, take a look at all the interesting people, young and old, who hang out on the plaza in front. It's a favorite place for street performers. On any given day, especially in the summer, you can watch fire-eaters, mimes,

musicians, and jugglers. Watch out, though, for pickpockets. It's their favorite place, too.

The Industrial Design Center is on the ground floor, where you'll find a permanent show on modern architecture. The third floor is home to the National Museum of Modern Art and its collection of paintings by some of this century's greatest artists. Many of them lived and worked in the studios of Paris.

Just to give you an idea, here are a few names you might recognize: Pablo Picasso, Salvador Dali, and Marc Chagall. As for American artists, you'll see abstract paintings by Jackson Pollock and sculpture by Alexander Calder, plus the pop art of Andy Warhol, who is well known for his huge Campbell soup cans.

After you've seen the exhibits, hop back onto the escalator for the fifth floor. There, you can catch a beautiful broad view of Paris rooftops and look down on the swarms of people who frequent this lively part of the city.

The next place to head for is the **Forum des Halles**. The best way to reach it is along the rue Berger. This whole area is a pedestrian mall so you don't have to worry about cars.

On the way, check out the **Fountain of the Innocents**. It's more than four hundred years old and sits on a spot that used to be a large cemetery dating back to the twelfth century. In the late 1700s, two million skeletons were dug up (you can now visit those bones underground in the Catacombs near the Place Denfert-Rochereau).

Farther on, you can't miss the Forum. It looks like a futuristic space station, with its white steel and glass sections that fan out like palm trees or fountains. Inside is a huge shopping mall that runs several levels underground. You'll find a store for just about everything at the Forum, including jeans, T-shirts, perfume, hats, candy, and music.

Parisians have been shopping on this spot for close to 900 years, when this was a huge outdoor food market. The Forum as you see it today was built during the 1980s.

Inside the Forum, on Level 1, be sure to visit the new **Musée Grévin**. It's an incredible wax museum, with animated life-size dolls that tell the history of Paris during one of its best periods, from 1885 to 1900. The 40-minute "sound and light" narration is usually in French, so be sure to ask them to play the English version.

During the show, you'll pass from room to room. One minute you're standing next to Gustav Eiffel as he talks about the revolutionary tower he's planning to build and the next you're watching Parisians sing and dance in the cabarets of Montmartre!

From the Forum head back toward the Fountain of the Innocents and take a right on the rue St. Denis. This street has been a very busy place since the seventh century. That's almost 1,300 years ago!

From this mix of the modern and ancient, let's head for one of the oldest and most charming neighborhoods in Paris. **Le Marais** spreads from the rue Beaubourg east of the Pompidou Center to the Place de la Bastille over ten blocks away.

Marais means "swamp" in French. During the early years of Paris no one could live in this area because it was basically underwater. But in the 1200s, as soon as Jesuit monks filled the swamp with dirt, the nobility began to move in and build mansions on the new land.

The best way to get to know the Marais is by just wandering along twisting narrow sidewalks next to the narrow cobblestone streets and alleys. Look at quirky things like old signs hanging over shops and ornate stone carvings around each door, peek into private courtyards, and have lunch at Jewish delis or Arab falafel stands.

Talk about stepping back in time. It's the exact opposite of the Eiffel Tower and Pompidou

St. Denis was an early Christian who, in A.D. 285, at the age of 90, had his head cut off for his religious beliefs. The story goes that Denis then picked up his head, washed it off in a fountain, and carried it 2,000 steps to the spot where the Basilica St. Denis is now built!

Watch for old street names in the Marais. Like the Rue des Mauvais Garçons, which means Bad Boys' Street, or Rue des Quatre Fils, Four Sons' Street!

Center and feels the way you might imagine the old Old World to be.

If you're in the mood for a good museum, try the **Hôtel Carnavelet** at 23, rue de Sévigné. This Renaissance mansion is all about the history of Paris and filled with great stuff left over from the palaces of kings and queens as well as the French Revolution.

A few of the streets, including the rue St.-Antoine and the rue Francois-Miron, were once old Roman highways that cut through the swamp, bringing soldiers and merchants to Paris long ago.

On the east side of the Marais is the **Place de la Bastille** where rebels tore down an awful old prison, called the Bastille, in 1789. It took them no time at all to pull down every stone and then start the French Revolution. Today, the site of the prison is marked out with stones on the sidewalk, to show you where it once stood.

As a contrast, take a look at the brand-new glass opera house on the square. It's called the **Opéra de Paris Bastille**, and it will probably remind you of the futuristic architecture of the Pompidou Center and the Pyramid at the Louvre.

4. A City Is Born

The river Seine flows gently through the heart of Paris, neatly dividing it into the Left Bank and the Right Bank. The Left is basically the bottom section on your map, and the Right is on top.

There's a romantic story about how the Gauls, a barbarian tribe that first inhabited the area, believed the tears of a river goddess were the source of the Seine, 150 miles to the south of Paris. In any case, the Seine is 500 miles long and travels far north to the English Channel. It's also one of the world's most famous rivers.

Take a walk across one of the Seine's fourteen bridges in Paris. Near the center of the city, look down at the river and you'll see many old barges lined up one after the other. They're moored to big steel rings that have been attached to the Seine's stone bank for centuries.

Watch a barge come floating down the river with one of the crew members swabbing the broad flat deck. It might be carrying lightweight cargo, such as fruits and vegetables, or its owners might just be out taking a pleasure cruise.

If you want to see what Paris looks like from their perspective, take a trip on one of the pleasure boats that cruise up the river. Day or night,

In A.D. 451, Attila the Hun was on his way to invade Paris with 700,000 men and the Parisians began to flee. But a young girl, Genevieve, told them God would save the city. Nobody knows why, but Attila did change his mind and switch his course. Parisians called it a miracle and made Genevieve a saint!

Visit the squawking bird markets every Sunday at the Place Louis Lépine on the Île de la Cité and every day except Sunday along the Quai de la Mégisserie.

these guided trips are super. They have several pick-up locations near the islands. Take your pick! They each have glass sides and roofs to give you an amazing perspective of the Paris of yesterday and today.

Back on land, head straight for the **Île de la Cité** on which the Cathedral of Notre Dame was built. This little island in the middle of the Seine is where civilization began in Paris, back in the 3rd century B.C.—more than 2,100 years ago!

The island was called Lutece back then, and six thousand people lived on and around it. A Gallic tribe of fishermen called the Parisii built their community on the island because it could be protected from enemies. Roman soldiers settled in the area south of the Seine.

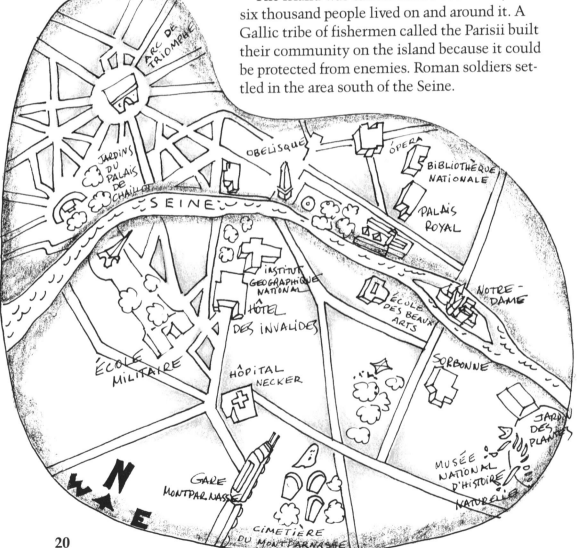

Second only to the Eiffel Tower, the **Cathedral of Notre Dame** is the best-known landmark in Paris. It took almost two hundred years to build this huge Gothic church, from 1163 to 1345. Gothic simply means it was designed with pointed arches, rib vaulting, and flying buttresses because that was the architectural style of the twelfth through the fifteenth centuries. Every skilled person in Paris pitched in to build the cathedral, including every stonemason and carpenter in town.

Many kings and queens and even the Emperor Napoleon were crowned here. The French writer, Victor Hugo, also made the church famous when he wrote *The Hunchback of Notre Dame* in the 1840s. When you visit the new Grévin wax museum in the Forum des Halles, Hugo will tell you more about his romantic novel and its tragic King Kong-like hero, Quasimodo.

Before you enter the cathedral, head down into the archaeological crypt beneath the square.

Paris has two Grévin wax museums, the new one at the Forum and the old one on the Boulevard Montmartre, not far from the Opéra. Check out the Musée Grévin for a realistic look at French and world history!

There, you'll see what remains of the early Parisii and Roman settlements, plus the foundation of a children's home. You probably have never seen structures as old as these. It's amazing to realize they survived this long.

Now, look at the front of the cathedral itself. Notice there are three huge portals with two enormous doors in each. Within and above the portals, you'll see carved statues of important figures from biblical and French history. In the center of the facade are the delicate stained glass panes of the Rose Window, which measures thirty feet across.

The cathedral is crowned with two huge rectangular towers. A 13-ton bell is in the tower to the right, but it only tolls these days when something terrible happens. In Victor Hugo's book, which takes place during the Middle Ages, it was the hunchback's job to ring the bell. At the Grévin wax museum, you'll see Quasimodo doing just that.

You can visit the towers through an outside entrance on the left side of the church. There, you'll climb up 386 steep steps and get a fantastic view of the cathedral's graceful architecture. You'll also get a close-up look at the great bell and tour a video-museum for more information on the cathedral's rich history.

Visitors have always been fascinated by the bizarre carved gargoyles that seem to gaze down at the busy city with some amusement, as if they're wondering what all those funny human beings are doing running around like crazy. Unfortunately, during the eighteenth century, after 600 years perched on the edge of the cathedral, some of the grotesque statues got too curious, leaned too far over, and smashed down head first to the pavement. Those that didn't fall were removed and replaced with new ones a hundred years ago.

Now you're ready to enter the enormous cathedral, which can hold 6,500 people during a

mass. Look at how the sunlight filters through the tall, brilliantly colorful stained glass windows. Some of them were made almost 800 years ago.

A huge, ancient organ above the main entrance has 110 stops. Every Sunday, beginning at 5:45 p.m., you can sit in the nave (the front section) and hear an organist play ancient and modern sacred music. It makes a powerful impression as the loud, crashing notes fill the immense stone hall.

France is very proud of the beauty of its ancient churches. Perhaps the most beautiful of them all is the Gothic masterpiece, **La Sainte-Chapel**. The chapel opened in the year 1248 just two blocks from Notre-Dame. Here you'll find the oldest stained glass windows in Paris. Each pane seems to glow when sunlight passes through it. Together the thousands of little pieces of colored glass re-create the stories of the Bible.

From the chapel, walk along the *quais*, or banks, heading around the island toward the back of the cathedral of Notre-Dame. As you're getting close to the tip of the island, you'll see the Square Jean XXIII—a nice place to have a picnic. It's right behind the cathedral, so you'll have a perfect view of the church's architecture, especially the flying buttresses and rib vaulting, from the back.

A little bit farther, on the very tip of the island, you'll find the **Deportation Memorial**, which was built to remember the two hundred thousand French citizens, most of whom were Jewish, who died in German concentration camps during World War II.

Just a stone's throw upstream from the Île de la Cité is the Seine's smallest island, the **Île St. Louis**. Cross over on the Pont St. Louis and you'll see some of the prettiest buildings in all of Paris.

Many of the city's oldest buildings were torn down during the late 1800s when Baron Haussmann reshaped and rebuilt so many of the neighborhoods, but most of the Île St. Louis was saved from that major demolition. This makes it seem like a little sanctuary from the hectic pace of the rest of the city, and you can enjoy a sense of stepping back in a time long before cars and television.

You can also taste the most delicious ice cream in Paris, at Berthillon, 31, rue St.-Louis-en-l'Île, except not during the month of August because that's when the owners and workers go on vacation. In fact, that's when most Parisians take off for the country or the coast and leave the city to visitors!

From 1940 until its liberation in August 1944, much of France, including Paris, was occupied by the Germans. Unlike most major European cities, it was not bombed by the Germans because a German general refused Hitler's orders to flatten it.

5. The Latin Quarter

From the Île St. Louis, cross over on the Pont de la Tournelle and you'll be back on the Left Bank. Take a right and walk along the quai in the direction of Notre-Dame. All along this sidewalk you'll pass the big open boxes of the booksellers perched on the wall. Keep an eye on what they're offering. You might spot a beautiful old postcard or poster of Paris to take home as a souvenir.

A few blocks down, on the rue de la Bucherie, you will see a sign for "Shakespeare & Co." on your left. This is the best-known English-language bookstore in Paris because many famous writers, including Ernest Hemingway, used to spend time here in the 1920s and 1930s. Today, it still looks a lot like it did sixty years ago. Drop by and check out the old shelves cluttered with used books. You might even find a beautiful old picture book of Paris.

Keep going along the quai until you come to the rue St. Jacques and then take a left. On your right you'll see the **rue de la Huchette**. It's the main street of a large and wonderful maze of narrow, old lanes left over from the medieval period.

No cars are allowed in this area, and you can watch people juggle flaming torches, swallow

In 53 B.C., the Roman leader Julius Caesar (he wasn't emperor yet) led his troops to subdue the rebellious Gallic tribes living along the Seine. But the stubborn Parisii fought hard against the Romans and finally burned their own city to the ground, rather than let Caesar's troops have it.

fire, or sing ballads with a guitar. If you're hungry, check out the many little restaurants serving Greek, Arab, Chinese, Italian, and Japanese food. This is also a great place to find vendor carts sizzling with Parisian crepes.

This whole area, for blocks and blocks heading south beyond the Boulevard St. Germain, is full of French and foreign students racing from class to class at one of the many local universities and specialized colleges. Those who aren't in class are sitting in cafés studying, gossiping, or discussing the meaning of life.

You might even see some American kids who are taking classes in French language and culture at the famous Sorbonne, one of the first universities in Paris. In fact, thousands of students take a year off from their American colleges to study in Paris every year. Maybe you'll join them someday!

On the other side of the busy pedestrian area, you'll find the **Boulevard St. Michel**, which the students call the Boul'Mich, pronounced "bool meesh." Parisian high school and college students love comic books, which are published in France with hard covers, and you can usually buy them at a discount anywhere along the Boul'Mich. Their favorite cartoon character is "Asterix," a little Gallic soldier living on the coast of France in 50 B.C.

On the corner of the Boul'Mich and the Boulevard St. Germain you'll find the **Hôtel de Cluny** and its museum. Here you can see the ruins of old Roman baths that are nearly 2,000 years old. And every Wednesday, at 3:00 p.m., you can take a guided tour of the ancient warm water bath, the cold water bath, and the steam room. Back then, of course, the people didn't have private bathrooms in their homes, so everyone had to take a bath together!

27

The museum has twenty-four galleries brimming with items from the Middle Ages, but it's best known for the beautiful red and gold tapestries that were woven 400 to 500 years ago. Be sure to see "The Lady and the Unicorn" series in Room XIII on the first floor.

Keep heading south on the Boul'Mich and into the heart of the ancient Roman community, now the university district. Soon, on your left, you'll see the broad **Place de la Sorbonne**, which leads up to the great university. Back then, just like today, students didn't always pay attention to their teachers or do what they were told. Paris has a long history of rebellious students.

This is called the Latin Quarter, mostly because all classes were taught in Latin until the French Revolution in the late 1700s. Drop by the Sorbonne and peek into one of the big round

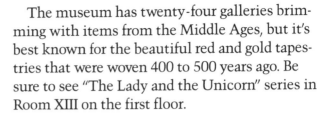

lecture halls where students sit on hard benches and take tons of notes, just like their ancestors did for centuries before them.

After the wild pace of the city, students and other Parisians like to head for the nearest park to meet friends, gossip, and catch some rays. Just a few blocks down on the Boul'Mich you'll find one of the city's greatest parks, the **Jardin du Luxembourg**. After soaking up so much Parisian history, let's see what's happening at the Luxembourg Gardens. Enter through the big gate on the Place E. Rostand.

If it's Sunday afternoon, there will definitely be a concert at the bandstand. It might be a big brass band or a small group of string players.

Take a look at the **Palais du Luxembourg**, which will appear on your right. After King Henri IV died in 1610, his queen, Marie de Medici, had the palace designed to remind her of the land where she grew up, the Italian region of Tuscany.

Unfortunately, the queen was not able to enjoy her palace for very long. She had some disagreements with the leader of the Catholic church, Cardinal Richelieu, and although her son was now King Louis XIII and should have protected her, she was sent off to Cologne where she died penniless.

Today, the royal garden is a vast playground for kids, parents, and grandparents. In the broad open area in front of the palace you'll find a large pond with a fountain. There, children and teenagers will be poking at toy sailboats that skim across the water's surface and bump into the ducks who don't pay much attention. Not far from the pool, you can rent a boat, too, for about ten francs an hour. Try it!

Visit the tip of the Île de la Cité to see its beautiful weeping willow. It's called the Vert Gallant, named after one of France's favorite kings, Henri IV.

Sunday is family day in France, and all the children and grandchildren are expected to arrive at Grandmaman's house for a huge dinner. It's an old tradition that most families still respect.

In addition to the puppet shows at Luxembourg Gardens, you'll find more marionettes at the Bois de Vincennes, at the corner of the avenues Matignon and Gabriel, and in the Champ-de-Mars near the Eiffel Tower.

Pass the pool and head up the steps into a park area shaded with chestnut trees. To the left, you'll see and hear kids playing on jungle jims and slides. If you have little brothers or sisters, let them loose in this little playground, or give them a push on the swings. Plus, there's a merry-go-round where everyone tries to hook the ring.

Right next to the carousel is the concession stand. Two of the most delicious Parisian snacks to try here are the waffles with whipped cream and chocolate and the cotton candy. Waffles are called *gaufres*, and they are soft and fat. The vendors put so much delicious cream and chocolate on them, it'll be hard to avoid getting some on your nose and cheeks. And watch them twirl the cotton candy out of sugar. The French call cotton candy *Barbe à Papa*, meaning "Daddy's Beard."

Right next to the concession is the marionette theater where you can sit in on a traditional puppet show, or *guignol* (geen-yol), Saturday afternoons at 4:00 and Sunday and Wednesday afternoons at 3:15 and 4:15.

Just before the show, a woman comes out and rings a loud hand-bell. Be sure you're in your seat for the 45-minute show. The puppeteers use old carved and painted puppets in a style that dates back centuries. You'll be watching the

same show Parisian children were watching in the 1800s, long before they could go to the movies!

In the other corner of the garden, next to the Palace, you'll find sweet little ponies that will let you ride on them for just a few francs!

Another favorite garden park for kids is the **Jardin des Plantes** on the far east side of the Latin Quarter, along the Seine. This is the city's first public zoo. It has a small selection of lions, tigers, monkeys, and reptiles. The garden is also well known for its fantastic collection of exotic birds, tropical and alpine plants, fossils, precious stones, and insects. Climb up the circular maze and get a great view of the whole garden.

A few blocks west of the Jardin des Plantes, you'll find what's left of a **Roman arena** that was destroyed by Barbarians in the year 280. Romans used to come to the arena and watch the circus and theater presentations!

The arena was buried for more than 1,500 years. It was discovered by accident when construction workers were trying to build a road over it. You can still see the old stage and wings of the arena, plus engraved stones that marked the reserved seats of the Roman leaders at the time.

The Rue Mouffetard is one of the oldest streets in Paris and was once part of the Roman road to Lyon. It's also a tiny street with tiny shops and restaurants. Step into this old world.

6. Napoleon Meets Mona Lisa

The **Louvre** is the largest royal palace in the world, and the museum inside it is the most famous. But it didn't start out that way. In the year 1200, King Philippe Auguste built a fortress on this spot where the city ended at that time. The fort was surrounded by a moat, to protect Paris from attack. Over the centuries, the Louvre grew into a palace for various royal families.

In October 1789, it became the perfect place for the rebels to put King Louis XVI, his wife, Marie-Antoinette, and their children when the revolution began. Parisians had finally become fed up with going hungry while their king and queen lived in luxury. The monarchy had the habit of putting on great dinners and balls for their friends while the general population starved to death in the streets.

In fact, life got so hard that the people didn't even have enough bread to eat. Unfortunately, when the queen heard this, she said, without thinking clearly, "Then, let them eat cake!" Well, if Parisians didn't have any bread, you can be sure they hadn't eaten cake in a very long time. That statement helped make the French mad enough to start the revolution, just a few years after the successful American Revolution.

Before universities were built, students had their classes outdoors and sat on bundles of straw.

In 1793, the king and queen were brought to a guillotine set up at the Place de la Concorde, not far from the Louvre, and had their heads cut off, which was a common way to execute criminal leaders in France. This was the start of a bloody Reign of Terror that didn't stop until nearly 1,400 people had gone to the scaffold.

Despite all the turmoil, the Louvre had begun to collect some of its masterpieces back in the early 1500s. For example, that's when King François I acquired Leonardo da Vinci's Mona Lisa, which is probably the most famous painting in the world. See if you can figure out why!

For a side trip, stroll up the Avenue de l'Opéra, leading from the Palais Royal near the Louvre. You'll come to the magnificent opera house, built in 1875 and home to some of the finest opera, dance, and concert performances in the world.

Today, the Louvre has more than 300,000 pieces in its collection. One of its most popular attractions today is the huge glass pyramid that architect I. M. Pei designed for the **Cour Napoleon**, the Louvre's central courtyard. After the Eiffel Tower and the Pompidou Center, this is a favorite spot for American kids.

The pyramid is now the main entrance to the Louvre, and you might think it looks out of place at first. After all, it's a mesh of tubes, cables, and sheet glass next to the carved stone walls of the Louvre.

The pyramid is surrounded on the outside by three smaller pyramids and pools filled with constantly running water and fountains. Enjoy sitting on the edge of the pools, especially on a hot day, when the clear water will keep you cool. And by standing in front of the pyramid, facing away from the courtyard, you should be able to see through the small Arc de Triomphe, past the obelisk of La Concorde, all the way up the

Champs-Elysées and glimpse the main Arc de Triomphe.

A curving staircase will take you under the pyramid and into a big bright hall with a reception and information desk, a bookshop, an auditorium, and an expensive cafeteria. A good way to profit from the Louvre is to take a guided tour in English which you can join on this basement level. The main entrance is through the Porte Sully into the Cour Carrée, part of the original Louvre fortress.

Or, if you go on your own, start at the ground level. Take a right toward the Pavillon des Arts for a look at the Venus de Milo, a headless but famous female statue that was carved during the height of Greek civilization, more than three thousand years ago. On the Daru Stairway leading to the first floor, pass by the soaring majestic form of the Winged Victory of Samothrace, which is also Greek but even older than the Venus.

In 1429, Joan of Arc led her troops to attack Paris and free the city from the English. When she was wounded by an arrow, her men retreated.

Also on the first floor, visit the most famous work of art in the world, Leonardo da Vinci's moody and mysterious portrait of Mona Lisa, painted during the Renaissance period in the early 1500s. You'll most likely have to stand in line for this magnificent painting because it is so very popular. When you do find yourself in front of the quietly smiling Mona Lisa, notice how da Vinci harmoniously blended the shapes and colors of the figure with her background.

There are also many other masterpieces in these rooms: paintings from early Dutch, Spanish, English, and German artists which will give you a super idea of how people lived back then and the different painting styles that were used to portray them. Remember, there were no cameras, so these are the only images we have of our European ancestors!

In the Galerie d'Apollon you can visit the priceless Crown Jewels and the enormous Regent diamond. These incredible gems, surrounded by gold and silver, are the best of what was once owned by those kings and queens who were thrown out during the French Revolution, precisely because they spent more money on jewelry than on the people.

And don't miss the huge halls full of Egyptian, Roman, and Greek art and sculpture. If you love art and history, you could spend a week in the Louvre and hardly see everything!

Now, if you need some fresh air after viewing all these masterpieces, take your time on a long walk toward the **Champs-Elysées** (pronounce it "shohns-aleezay") from the Louvre.

The first monument you'll see is the **Arc de Triomphe du Carroussel**, a small version of the great Arc de Triomphe at the head of the Champs-Elysées. The arch was built to celebrate Napoleon's victories in the early 1800s. From a short distance, look up at the top of the arch to see a goddess and the Winged Victory riding together in a chariot led by four horses.

Cross the avenue and walk into the formal gardens of the **Tuileries**. Its name is based on the word *tuiles* ("tile"), because five hundred years

ago this area is where workers dug up clay to make tiles. It was also once a huge garbage dump. Today, it's a beautiful escape from traffic and noise.

Farther on in the garden, you'll come to an eight-sided pond and a fountain. Here, as in the Jardin du Luxembourg, you can rent little boats and sail them in the pool. In the early summer, there's often a carnival in the garden.

Pass the basin and head toward the obelisk and two flanking fountains of the Place de la Concorde. This is one of the craziest and busiest intersections in Paris, so be very careful when you cross over to the obelisk.

Basically, an obelisk is a pillar that tapers into a pyramid at the top. And that's appropriate because the 75-foot monument was created in Egypt more than three thousand years ago. This, the oldest monument in Paris, is made of pink marble, weighs more than 220 tons, and is carved with hieroglyphic ducks, owls, and locusts. (Hieroglyphics was the written language of ancient Egypt.) It's been standing in the very same spot since 1836, when it was unloaded from a barge. Imagine, from the desert of Egypt to the banks of the Seine . . .

The **American Embassy** is on the Place de la Concorde, to the left of the Hôtel Crillon. This is where you would go if you lost your passport. The French and other non-Americans must apply at the embassy for a visa to visit the United States.

Check out the dark blue caps and broad-legged stance of the police, called *gendarmes* in France, who are keeping guard in front of the embassy and all along the Champs-Elysées.

The first half of this great sloping avenue is lined with a park of chestnut trees and a few concession stands for ice cream and other snacks during the warm months. The second half of the Champs-Elysées is the best known and busiest. It's lined with great buildings whose huge windows show off travel destinations, the latest cars, the latest movies, and the latest fashions.

By the way, the name "Champs-Elysées" means Elysian Fields in English. It's a place in Greek mythology where life is delightful for the blessed. See how you feel!

Until the early 1600s, this whole area was just open meadows and marsh where cows grazed and bandits hid out waiting for victims. In 1616, the queen, Marie de Medici, the same one who later built the palace at Luxembourg and died without a franc to her name, created a long avenue here which Parisians used for a Sunday "cruise" in their elegant carriages. Since then, it's been used for many events, including circuses, dances, concerts, and whatever other entertainment fun-loving Parisians could dream up!

If you're lucky enough to be in Paris on July 14, you can celebrate the French Independence Day, here on the Champs-Elysées. They call it Bastille Day and there will be huge crowds

Paris has a museum for just about everything: eyeglasses and binoculars, hunting, locks, things counterfeit, stamps, posters, and wine!

watching musical and military parades and jets streaming overhead. And if you're there about a week later, watch the winners of one of the biggest bike races in the world, the Tour de France, ride into the finish line on the Champs-Elysées.

For some of the best fireworks displays in the world, try to get near **Trocadero**, near the Eiffel Tower, on the night before Bastille Day. And on the night of July 14, starting at 10:00, watch the megawatt light show when a laser will shoot through the Arc de Triomphe all the way to the Grande Arche de La Défense. If you can't get close because of the crowds, find a high spot anywhere in Paris and watch the incredible live special effects!

You'll also find several good museums at the Rond-Point des Champs-Elysées. Like the Eiffel Tower, the **Grand Palais** and **Petit Palais** were built for the 1900 World Exhibition. When you visit one of their permanent or temporary art gallerys, notice the architecture of stone, steel, and glass.

If you like science museums, step into the **Palais de la Découverte** for exhibits on astronomy, optics, and nuclear physics. Unfortunately, most of the explanations are only in French, although its wonderful planetarium show is in the universal language of the stars!

Stroll on up the Champs-Elysées and be ready to be bumped around by swarms of Parisians and tourists from all over the world. You might even feel like a fish swimming upstream, although the sidewalks are the widest in Paris. At numbers 64 and 84, you'll find huge indoor shopping malls, and all along the avenue, you'll find cafés and restaurants whose little round tables and umbrellas spill out into your path.

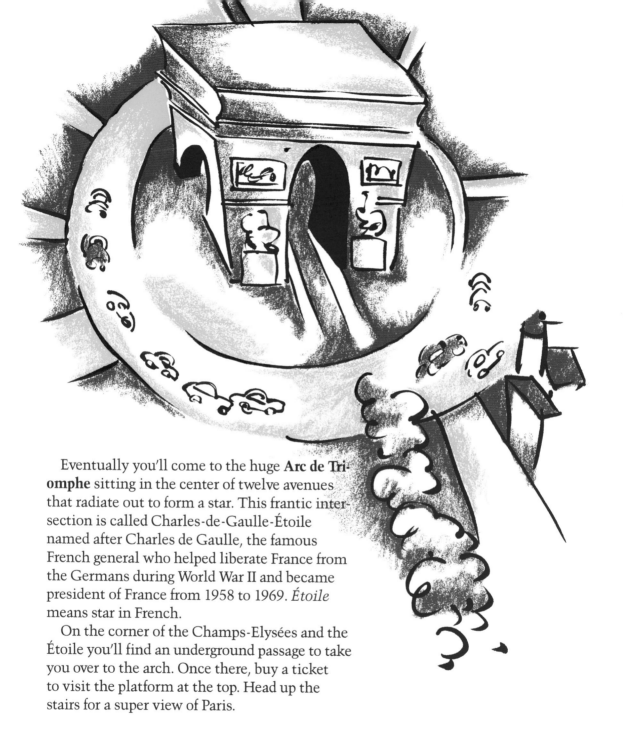

Eventually you'll come to the huge **Arc de Triomphe** sitting in the center of twelve avenues that radiate out to form a star. This frantic intersection is called Charles-de-Gaulle-Étoile named after Charles de Gaulle, the famous French general who helped liberate France from the Germans during World War II and became president of France from 1958 to 1969. *Étoile* means star in French.

On the corner of the Champs-Elysées and the Étoile you'll find an underground passage to take you over to the arch. Once there, buy a ticket to visit the platform at the top. Head up the stairs for a super view of Paris.

Not far from the Eiffel Tower, you'll find the École Militaire, or Military School. When Napoleon Bonaparte graduated from the school in 1787 at the age of 18, his teachers said he would "go far." In fact, he went so far as to try and conquer the world!

In 1806, Emperor Napoleon commissioned an architect to design and build the giant arch. He wanted a monument to honor the French soldiers who were helping him win so many battles on his conquest of Europe. Unfortunately, the other European countries, and especially England, were getting fed up with Napoleon's invasions and eventually defeated and exiled the emperor to the island of St. Helena, where he died long before the arch was finished. The French were heartbroken and spent years trying to get his body back.

One snowy winter day in 1840, twenty years after his death, a chariot slowly and mournfully carried Napoleon's body through the arch on its way to the Invalides for burial in a magnificent tomb. Some French still boast about Napoleon's ambition and victories, never forgetting the country's great years of military glory.

The arch measures 164 feet high and 148 feet wide and is carved with hundreds of figures from French history. In 1920, an Unknown Soldier was buried in a special tomb beneath the arch. Every evening at 6:30, you can watch old veterans come and light the eternal flame at his grave, paying their respects to all those Frenchmen who died anonymously on native and foreign battlefields.

France was once a great world power. It ruled many colonies throughout Africa, the Caribbean, and Southeast Asia and was in constant rivalry with its European neighbors for global supremacy. Carved into the stone sides of the arch you'll find the names of the country's favorite battles during the Empire of Napoleon, plus the names of 558 of Napoleon's generals.

At the end of World War I and then World War II, thousands of victorious soldiers marched through the arch and down the Champs-Elysées to the cheers of thousands of grateful Parisians. The arch is a great place to celebrate a victory, and you can watch a film showing some of those incredible events in a small museum located inside. One guy even tried to fly a small plane through it, just to see if he would fit. (Find out if he did!)

The French president's home and office is called the Palais de l'Elysée, and it's surrounded by high stone walls. Walk by on the corner of Avenue de Marigny and Rue du Faubourg St. Honoré.

7. Montmartre

s you wander around Paris, you'll notice a hill to the north of the city with a gleaming white dome sitting on top of it. The hill is **Montmarte**, and the dome belongs to the basilica of **Sacre-Coeur**, a Roman Catholic church built in 1900, the same year the subway opened. Since Montmartre is the highest natural point in the city, it's one of the best spots for a full view of the skyline. On a clear day, you'll see for at least 30 miles, far above the rooftops of Paris.

There are a few ways to get to the peak of this little mountain. There's the tram, or *funiculaire*, which looks like a ski gondola. You can hop on at the station to the left of the broad stairs that lead up to the Sacre-Coeur.

Or you can walk up those white sandstone stairs, stopping here and there to turn and catch the view of Paris. Better yet, you can hike up one of the narrow, steep cobblestone stairways that Parisians have been using for centuries.

If you do take the stairway, you will cross the many old streets that zigzag their way up to the crest and get a taste of what life has been like on this hill for many generations. Imagine, too, that the early Celtic tribesmen, and the Romans,

Montmartre did not officially become part of Paris until 1860. Before then, and even since, people leaving the "Butte" said they were "going down to Paris."

used to worship their gods here long before the birth of Jesus.

Most people head straight for the **Place du Tertre** as soon as they reach the top. You can't miss the little square because it's crammed with artists and their easels surrounded by cafés and restaurants. The artists will try very hard to get you to sit down so they can do a sketch or caricature of you. Many of them are talented and will give you a good picture to hang on your wall at home.

One way to see what Montmartre is all about is to take a 40-minute ride on a little white mini-train that tours the back streets. You can catch it just on the edge of the Place du Tertre. It's a slow, bumpy but fun ride back into the Bohemian and tumultuous history of what the local people call the *Butte.*

The side streets of Mont-martre are often bustling with open markets. Pari-sians bring their own sacks and go to separate shops for meat, bread, cheese, fruit and vegeta-bles, and flowers. Mmmm . . . enjoy the aroma!

A few blocks from the Place du Tertre, in the rue Poulbot, drop by the **Montmartre Wax Museum**, with its many rooms full of life-size wax dolls that look like they could come alive and reach out to touch you.

One of the best-known figures there is Henri de Toulouse-Lautrec. He was a famous artist in the late nineteenth century who painted the colorful dancers and singers of Montmartre on some of the first posters ever made.

The rue Poulbot was named after a Monsieur Poulbot who liked to draw pictures of the children who played and sometimes lived in the street during the early 1900s. You can see sam-ples of his drawings of wide-eyed kids with mis-chievous grins at the **Maison Poulbot** located at 3, Place du Tertre. If you want to take one home, some of the souvenir shops around the square also sell postcards and posters of the Poulbot street urchins.

Even though the square is usually crammed with tourists, you can still see many reminders of old Paris. For example, coming out of one cor-ner you might hear the tinkling notes of an organ grinder singing some beautiful old cabaret songs. While the singer is grinding the organ to keep the music going, a monkey wearing a little cap and jacket might be holding a cup for you to drop coins into. Go ahead, don't be shy!

8. From Trains to Fine Art

The **Musée d'Orsay** used to be the Gare d'Orsay—a train station! Architects and builders spent six years transforming it into a fantastic museum of art, and finally it opened its doors in 1986. The first thing you'll notice is the original glass ceiling that lets plenty of filtered natural light pour down on a central hallway full of sculptures.

The museum offers tons of special activities for children and workshops on the museum's great collection of paintings, photographs, music, sculpture, silent movies, books, furniture, and buildings. Everything here was created between the years 1848 and 1914. It's wonderful! The information people all speak English and will help you get involved.

As you wander through the museum's beautiful halls, notice the great range of style, technique, and subject matter used by romantic, impressionist, realist, classicist, and early symbolist painters. Nearly all of the artists here are French, but you will see *The Mother*, painted by American artist James Whistler. Like the Mona Lisa, this image of an old woman seated stiffly in profile is very famous. You might even recognize it!

One of the most popular artists today is Vincent van Gogh, who actually died penniless in 1890. He was Dutch but for many years lived on Montmartre and in the south of France. He never sold a single painting during his lifetime, but a few years ago someone paid more than $80 million for one of his works in New York. It was the highest price anyone had ever paid for a painting!

On the upper level of the museum, you'll find entire rooms full of van Gogh paintings. Take a look and see what you think of this tragic master.

Some people can spend a whole day here because there is so much to see and think about, but if you'd like to get out on the street again, head over to the **Invalides**. You can reach it through the lawns of the Esplanade that begin at the Pont Alexandre III. By the way, check out the incredible gold sculpture on the Alexandre bridge.

Invalides means people who are injured or handicapped. The name is appropriate because King Louis XIV had the buildings constructed to take care of wounded veterans. Head around to the Dome Church section in which Napoleon was buried after his body was returned from exile.

The crypt, designed just to hold Napoleon's tomb, is an awesome round hall lined with columns and statues. In the middle of the marble room is a red sarcophagus on a base of green granite. Beneath it all are six small coffins that hold Napoleon's body, along with two silver vessels that contain his heart and stomach. Strange, but this was how the French showed their respect for him.

9. Atoms, Animals, and More Tombs

Many buildings in this neighborhood were the townhouses of French nobility. Today, they serve as government offices of the embassies of Switzerland, Sweden, and Italy.

Let's get off the beaten track and check out the eastern fringe of Paris.

Start at the massive new science center called **La Villette**, or the City of Science and Industry. You can reach it by taking the Métro to Porte de la Villette. Or, if you have extra time, get off the subway at Jean-Jaurès and ride a canal boat to the science center. Boats usually run every half hour on weekends and holidays.

La Villette opened in 1986, and it's already a mecca for Parisian children, adults, and foreign visitors. You'll have a great time playing with the hundreds of hands-on exhibits set up to share the most important scientific discoveries with you. And many of them are also in English.

The main building is called Explora. Here you can wander into outer space, into submarines, and through the human brain. Chat with a robot, check out your eyesight, and test your sense of smell. Plus, explore the qualities of light and the natural environment of Earth. Rent a pair of headsets for more information on hundreds of topics.

Check out the planetarium, on Level 2 of Explora, with its already famous intergalactic

shows called "Children of the Sun" and "The Adventures of Starball."

Then head for the Géode, an enormous steel globe sitting in a square pool of water. You will be amazed at this huge shiny ball with the sky and the neighborhood reflected clearly in its mirrored panels.

Stroll right into the Géode and take a seat in the auditorium for an incredible Omnimax show on a curved screen. Fifty different films are shown in the Géode on just about every science topic you can think of. You will not want to miss one!

After La Villette, for a change of pace, take the Nation subway and get off at **Père-Lachaise** for one of the funkiest cemeteries you'll ever walk through.

For example, if you know much about the history of rock-and-roll music, you might remember Jim Morrison, the lead singer of The Doors. Well, he's buried here, in a tomb that American and Parisian students often visit. In fact, they've scribbled his name with arrows on other tombs to show their friends the way. At the cemetery entrance, you can pick up a guide that tells you where to find the tombs of famous people.

It's hard to imagine that a cemetery could be fun, but here you'll walk by strange statues, including a life-size ballerina, a pelican, plus plenty of angels, dogs, and mythological creatures. Some of the great writers and artists of American and European history are also buried here, including France's favorite singer, Edith Piaf. The cemetery is also bird and cat heaven. You'll see why!

After a visit to the cemetery, let's head for the **Vincennes Zoo** (get off at Porte Dorée), the largest zoo in France. It's located within the vast Bois de Vincennes, which was once a royal forest where only the king and his friends were allowed to hunt.

On your way to the zoo (follow the signs for "Parc Zoologique"), you'll see a small lake. If you're hungry, rent a canoe and picnic on the water. Beside the lake, you can also sit on the grass for lunch; in the zoo, it's tables only.

The zoo is home to more than 550 mammals and 700 birds of about 200 different species! And they all live in environments that come pretty close to their natural habitat. In fact, there's a huge artificial rock in the middle of the zoo just for those wild mountain sheep who love to climb steep cliffs.

Next to the Invalides, in the rue de Varenne, you'll find the **Rodin Museum**, *dedicated to Auguste Rodin, one of France's most famous sculptors. Check out the sculpture garden and one piece you may recognize:* The Thinker.

Walk along shaded and sunny paths observing the behavior of wild animals native to every corner of the world: from the Arctic, Africa, South America, North America, Australia, and tropical zones. See polar bears, giraffes, jaguars, otters, elephants, gazelles, and kangaroos. And don't miss the giant rocky cave habitat where hundreds of primates, including baboons, run and play, or the broad grassy field where lions snooze in the sun.

Deeper into the park, you'll find the 75 acres of the **Parc Floral de Paris** filled with different blossoms year-round. Also, during July and August, singers, musicians, actors, and clowns come out to perform. But best of all, there's a miniature golf course. It's laid out like Paris with the Seine running through it and holes called Notre-Dame and Sacre-Coeur!

Following up on your trek to the zoo, drop by the **Museum of African and Oceanian Arts**, just outside the park's border, near the Porte Dorée Métro. It has an awesome tropical aquarium; Parisian kids drop by especially for the crocodiles.

10. Skeletons Don't Swim

The Disney people are planning to build a French Disneyland west of Paris. It should open in 1992 with typical Disney characters, like Blanche Neige, or Snow White.

Back on the edge of the west side of Paris, you'll find the more than two thousand acres of the **Bois de Boulogne**. Long ago, this vast wood was full of bears, deer, wolves, and wild boars, which the local people hunted. But so many robbers liked hanging out in it, waiting for victims to ride by, that King Henri II had a wall built around the forest in 1556. Today, it's a great place to relax. There's plenty of space to play, bike, ride horses, and take a long walk.

The first place to visit is on the northeast edge of the Bois. It's the children's amusement park, called the **Jardin d'Acclimatation**, near the Porte des Sablons. It's got a track for racing miniature cars and motorcycles, plus a miniature golf course, a bowling alley, and a giant doll's house. There's also a small zoo, a theater, and plenty of open space for frisbee!

Just outside the children's park, you'll find a place to rent a bicycle, or even a bicycle built for two, called a tandem. Because the wood is so big and there are so many great parts to see, the best way to get around is on a bike. Ask for a bike map and head out for a leisurely ride along the winding paths.

One of the most famous flea markets in the world is located at Porte de Clignancourt. Two thousand sellers will offer you everything from pure junk to a possible masterpiece!

For example, ride down to the Lac Inférieure, or Lower Lake, and rent a boat for an hour. Or ride over to the Pré Catalan and stop at the two children's playgrounds on each side of the meadow. Not far west of the Pré Catalan you'll find the Grande Cascade, a beautiful man-made waterfall. And if you like flowers, visit the **Parc de Bagatelle** where in May you'll see irises in bloom, from June to October the roses, and in August the water lilies!

The Bois is one place where old-timers and young people too like to get together for a game of *boules*. You'll see them standing around very seriously discussing a collection of silver balls on the ground and occasionally throwing one. It's a game of precision that looks like a cross between bowling and pool. Go ahead and watch, the players concentrate so hard they probably won't even notice you.

Not far from Bagatelle, cross the Seine on the Pont de Neuilly, walk up the steps, and enter into a futuristic neighborhood. This is called **La Défense**, and it's an incredible collection of colorful fantasy-like towers designed to house apartments and offices.

Many of the towers are round or S-shaped, painted with varying shades of blue, green, and yellow and pierced with tiny windows cut in odd places. Some of them might remind you of a big chunk of Swiss cheese or a giant's toy set.

Walk through the Défense complex until you arrive at the **La Grande Arche**. This is actually a gigantic square created out of glass and marble and would weigh 300,000 tons if you could get it on a scale. Also, if you could lift the Cathedral of Notre-Dame, it would fit perfectly into the middle of the arch!

Take a ride up inside the glass walls for another great view of Paris from the top. The only landmark you won't see is the Eiffel Tower. It's blocked by the **Montparnasse Tower**, far on the other side of the river, which seems to shoot up out of nowhere from within an old artistic and working-class neighborhood on the Left Bank.

After the French Revolution, Montparnasse was the place for Parisians to sing and laugh in cafés and cabarets. Poets nicknamed the neighborhood long ago after a site in Greek history and mythology, Mount Parnassus.

Parisians love the beautiful park, Buttes-Chaumont, with its rolling hills, flower beds, a swan and duck pond, rocky cliffs, and waterfalls.

The Bois de Boulogne boasts two famous tracks for horseracing, the Hippodrome de Longchamp and the Hippodrome d'Auteuil. Longchamp also has a supervised playground with pony rides.

On April Fool's Day, in 1897, a group of musicians gave a concert for the Catacomb skeletons. But apparently it was disappointing. No one cheered.

Later, at the turn of this century, some of the world's greatest modern painters, writers, composers, poets, and thinkers lived and worked here, including Marc Chagall, Igor Stravinsky, Ernest Hemingway, and Lenin.

Most of what makes Montparnasse fun today is its nightlife for adults. But you can ride the elevator to the 59th floor and walk out on an open terrace, the highest in Paris. This is one of the best spots for a full view of the city.

Head down the Avenue du Maine toward the Montparnasse Cemetery (which you can visit if you're in the mood) and turn onto the rue Froidevaux. This is a nice shaded residential street that will take you toward the Place Denfert-Rochereau and the Catacombes.

Some people say the **Catacombes** are scary because they are a sort of underground burial place, called an ossuary. Not everyone has a good time walking through the long dark tunnels and small rooms in which human skulls and tibias (leg bones) have been neatly stacked up along the walls.

The skeletons were brought here from old cemeteries. Despite its reputation, there's always a long line of visitors waiting to get in, including small children and old folks. The halls are dimly lit, and some people like to bring their own flashlight. It's an unusual experience!

If you'd rather go swimming, take the Métro to the Balard stop and head for the sporting complex called **L'Aquaboulevard de Paris**. Buy a ticket for a four-hour swim in an enormous pool with long, winding slides, toboggans, sandy beaches, tropical islands, and a lagoon. Bring a bathing suit and a towel. Now you're all set to escape the city.

11. Outside Paris—A Palace and a Pond

I

France is a country bursting with castles and cathedrals, wines and cheese. To feel like a Parisian, don a beret and try a plate of snails!

f you've ever wondered what it would be like to live like a king or queen, a trip to the **Château de Versailles**, 12 miles southwest of Paris, will clue you in. More than 300 years old, this incredible palace was the center of French court life for more than a century, until the reign of Louis XVI basically put an end to the monarchy.

The palace took four years to build, from 1678 to 1682. Louis XIV was the first king to move in, transferring the entire court from the Louvre. Louis XIV was nicknamed the Sun King because his court artists and artisans were considered quite brilliant. For example, his royal gardener, André Le Nôtre, was the man who redesigned the Tuileries gardens into the classical style it has today.

Until Louis XIV's move away from the everyday life of Paris to the rich and secluded life of Versailles, the French were still somewhat tolerant of the spending habits of their kings. But when the king only returned to Paris from time to time for a banquet or parade, and didn't seem concerned at all by the needs of the people, some began to consider rebellion.

In 1789, when the mob finally overthrew the

Far to the southeast of Paris, you'll find the majestic Alps. Hikers and skiers love these enormous mountains that separate France from Switzerland and Italy.

monarchy, they hauled Louis XVI, grandson of Louis XIV, out of Versailles and brought him back to the Louvre where he was later executed. The palace is now a museum and park.

The palace of Versailles is an incredibly ornate example of French eighteenth-century taste. Visit the huge salons decorated in gold and velvet where the king and queen hosted many huge banquets and balls. Plus, you'll see the Hall of Mirrors and the king and queen's own separate suites. Bring a picnic, have lunch in the classical garden, and watch the beautiful one-hour musical fountain show, a water and light extravaganza the king ordered to entertain his friends.

France is well known for its many chateaus, or palaces, which were inhabited by members of the aristocracy for hundreds of years. There are many near Paris which are no longer residences and are now open to visitors. Imagine you're a duke or duchess and roam around your palace!

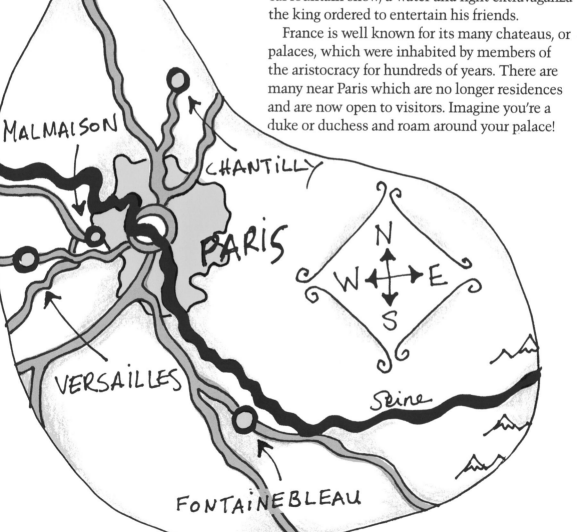

MALMAISON

CHANTILLY

PARIS

N
W E
S

VERSAILLES

Seine

FONTAINEBLEAU

Or, pretend you're visiting the Emperor Napoleon and his wife, Josephine, at their 250-year-old chateau in **Reuil-Malmaison**. He probably wouldn't be there, since Napoleon didn't like the chateau very much and spent most of his time in Paris plotting strategies for the conquest of Europe. But Josephine gave many parties here and changed her ball gowns often. After all, she had 600 of them!

The palace of **Fontainebleau** is located 30 miles south of Paris in the middle of a 41,000-acre forest. This palace is far older than Versailles or Malmaison. It was built more than 800 years ago. You can take a good long hike through the forest.

Chantilly is a chateau to the north of Paris, and if you know anything about whipped cream, this is where it's the most delicious. There's always a vendor parked right outside the chateau selling waffles piled high with chantilly whipped cream. The original chateau was built during the 1500s and is still surrounded by a moat.

Giverny is a charming country village where the waters of two rivers, the Epte and the Seine, meet and create a poetic setting that impressionist artist Claude Monet has made famous through his paintings. Visit the pond with the water lilies you often see in his works.

If you're in the mood for just pure fun, visit the Asterix Theme Park about 22 miles north of Paris in the village of Plailly. It's a total fantasy land for kids, with a Roman city equipped with an area for gladiators and chariots, a village made up to look like early Paris, and another one that looks like the Middle Ages. Plus, there are log rides, a roller coaster, a ghost train, a dolphin amphitheater, a magic cinema, and a musical banquet hall!

For a long trip out of Paris, visit Mont St. Michel on the Atlantic coast in the province of Normandy. It's a fairy-tale village, built on a hill of granite floating on a vast sea of quicksand!

French/English Glossary

French	English
Bonjour *(bonjhore)*	Hello
Au revoir *(oh revwar)*	Good-bye
S'il vous plaît *(seal voo play)*	Please
Merci *(mairsee)*	Thank you
Pardon *(pardohn)*	Excuse me
Ou est le Métro? *(oo ay le maytro?)*	Where is the metro?
Ou sont les toilettes? *(oo sohn lay twalet?)*	Where is the rest room?
Je suis perdu *(je swee peardoo)*	I am lost
Je m'appelle *(je mapelle)*	My name is. . .
Parlez-vous l'anglais? *(parlay voo longlay?)*	Do you speak English?
Je voudrais *(je voodray)*	I would like
des pommes frites *(day pom freet)*	some French fries
du lait *(doo lay)*	some milk
de la glace *(de la glasse)*	some ice cream
un sandwich *(uhn sondveech)*	a sandwich
de l'eau *(de low)*	some water
rue *(roo)*	street
musée *(myuzay)*	museum
bateau *(ba-toe)*	boat
ouvert *(oovare)*	open
fermé *(faremay)*	closed
le, la, les	the

Numbers 1-10

un *(uhn)*	one
deux *(de)*	two
trois *(twa)*	three
quartre *(kahtr)*	four
cinq *(sank)*	five
six *(seese)*	six
sept *(set)*	seven
huit *(hweet)*	eight
neuf *(nef)*	nine
dix *(deese)*	ten

The Details

American Embassy
2, avenue Gabriel
75008 Paris
42.96.12.02
Metro: Concorde

American Hospital
63, Boulevard Victor Hugo
92202 Neuilly-sur-Seine
(suburb)
47.47.53.00 or 46.41.25.25

Arc de Triomphe
Place de l'Etoile
75008 Paris
Open every day
43.80.31.31
Metro: Etoile

La Grande Arche
1, Parvis de la Defense
92040 Paris La Defense
Open every day
49.07.26.26
RER: La Defense (suburban
train)

Aquaboulevard de Paris Forest Hill
4-6, rue Louis Armand
75015 Paris
Open every day
40.60.10.00
Metro: Balard

Basilique du Sacre-Coeur
35, rue du Chevalier-de-la-Barre
75018 Paris
Open every day
42.51.17.02
Metro: Anvers

Bateaux Mouches (Seine rides)
Leave from Pont d'Alma
Paris 75008
Run every day
Metro: Alma Marceau

Bateaux Parisiens
Leave from Pont d'Iena
Paris 75007
Run every day
Metro: Trocadero

Bois de Boulogne
Metro: Porte Maillot

Canauxrama (Canal rides)
Bassin de la Villette
5 bis, Quai de la Loire
42.39.15.00
Metro: Jaures

Les Catacombes
2, Place Denfert-Rochereau
75014 Paris
Closed Monday and Friday
43.22.47.63
Metro: Denfert-Rochereau

La Cathédrale de Paris, Notre-Dame
Place du Parvis Notre Dame
75004 Paris
Open every day
Metro: Cite

Centre de la Mer et des Eaux (city aquarium)
195, rue St. Jacques
75007 Paris
Closed Monday
46.33.08.61
Metro: Pont Royal

Centre Georges Pompidou
rue St. Martin/Rue Beaubourg
75004 Paris
Closed Tuesday
42.77.12.33 or 42.77.11.12
Metro: Rambuteau

Château de Chantilly
Chantilly
Closed Tuesday

Château de Fontainebleau
Fontainebleau
Closed Tuesday

Château de Malmaison
1, avenue du Chateau
Reuil-Malmaison
Closed Tuesday
47.49.20.07
RER: La Défense and bus 158A

Château de Versailles
Place du Chateau
Versailles
Closed Monday and holidays
(gardens open every day)
30.84.74.00
RER: Versailles-Rive-Gauche
Cimetiere Pere-Lachaise
Metro: Pere Lachaise

Conciergerie (former prison during Revolution)
1, Quai de l'Horloge
75004 Paris
Open every day
43.54.30.06
Metro: Cite/Chatelet

Les Egouts de Paris (Paris sewers)
93, Quai d'Orsay
75007 Paris
Closed Thursday and Friday
47.05.10.29
Metro: Pont de l'Alma

Le Forum des Halles
Metro: Chatelet Les Halles

Le Grand Palais
3, avenue Winston Churchill
75008 Paris
Closed Tuesday
42.89.54.10
Metro: Champs-Elysees-Clemenceau

Hôtel des Invalides (Napoleon's tomb)
75007 Paris
Closed weekends
40.63.22.22
Metro: Varenne

Jardin d'Acclimatation
Metro: Sablons

Jardin du Luxembourg
Open every day
Metro: Odeon

Jardin des Plantes
(Natural History Museum)
57, rue Cuvier
75005 Paris
40.79.30.00
Open every day (museum closed Tuesday)
Metro: Jussieu or Monge

Maison de Victor Hugo
6, place des Vosges
75004 Paris
Closed Monday
42.72.10.16
Metro: Chemin Vert

Marché aux Puces (Flea Market)
75018 Paris
Open Saturday, Sunday and Monday only
Metro: Porte de Clignancourt

Musée de Cire de la Butte (Montmartre Wax Museum)
9 and 11, rue Poulbot
75018 Paris
46.06.78.92

Musée des Arts Africains et Océaniens
293, avenue Daumesnil
75012 Paris
Closed Tuesday
43.43.14.54
Metro: Porte Doree

Musée des Arts Decoratifs
107, rue de Rivoli
75001 Paris
Closed Monday, Tuesday and mornings
42.60.32.14
Metro: Palais Royal

Musée des Arts et Traditions Populaires (Folk Art Museum)
6, avenue du Mahatma-Gandhi
Bois de Boulogne
Closed Tuesday
40.67.90.00
Metro: Sablons

Musée des Arts de la Mode (Fashion Museum)
109, rue de Rivoli
75001 Paris
Closed Monday, Tuesday and mornings
42.60.32.14
Metro: Palais Royal

Musée Carnavalet
23, rue de Sevigne
75003 Paris
Closed Monday
42.72.21.13
Metro: St. Paul

Musée de Cluny
6, Place Paul-Painleve
75005 Paris
Closed Tuesday
43.25.62.00
Metro: St. Michel

Musée Grévin du Forum (animated wax museum)
Forum des Halles
75001 Paris
Open every day
40.26.28.50
Metro: Chatelet-Les-Halles

Musée du Louvre/Grand Pyramide
75001 Paris
Closed Tuesday
40.20.50.50
Metro: Palais Royal or Musee du Louvre

Musée de l'Homme (Museum of Mankind)
Palais de Chaillot
75016 Paris
Closed Tuesday and holidays
45.53.70.60
Metro: Trocadero

Musée de la Marine (Maritime Museum)
Palais de Chaillot
75016 Paris
Closed Tuesday
45.53.31.70
Metro: Trocadero

Musée de Montmartre
12, rue Cortot
75018 Paris
Closed Monday and mornings
46.06.61.11
Metro: Lamarck-Caulaincourt

Musée d'Orsay
1, rue de Bellechasse
75007 Paris
Closed Monday
40.49.48.14
Metro: Musee d'Orsay

Musée Picasso
5, rue de Thorigny
75003 Paris
Closed Tuesday
42.71.25.21
Metro: St. Paul

L'Opéra
1, Place de l'Opera
75009 Paris
47.42.57.50
Metro: Opera

Palais de la Découverte
Avenue Franklin D. Roosevelt
75008 Paris
Closed Monday
43.59.18.21 or 40.74.80.00
Metro: Franklin D. Roosevelt

Parc Asterix
60-Plailly
Open every day
(16) 44.60.60.00

Parc de Bagatelle
Route de Sevres
Metro: Pont de Neuilly

Parc Floral de Paris
Route de la Pyramide
75012 Paris
Open every day
Metro: Chateau de Vincennes,
then bus 112

Le Petit Palais
1, avenue Winston Churchill
75008 Paris
Closed Tuesday
42.65.12.73
Metro: Champs-Elysees-
Clemenceau

Sainte Chapelle
Boulevard du Palais
Located within the Palais de
Justice
75001 Paris
Open every day except some
major holidays
Metro: Cite

La Tour Eiffel (Eiffel Tower)
Quai Branly
75007 Paris
Open every day
45.55.91.11
Metro: Champ-de-Mars

La Tour Montparnasse
33, avenue du Maine
75015 Paris
45.38.32.32
Metro: Montparnasse-Bienvenue

Vedettes de Paris
Leave from Pont d'Iena
75015 Paris
Run every day
Metro: Bir Hakeim

**La Villette, Cité des Sciences et
de l'Industrie**
30, avenue Corentin-Cariou
75019 Paris
Closed Monday
40.05.72.72 or 46.42.13.13
Metro: Porte de la Villette

Zoo de Vincennes
Avenue Daumesnil
Open every day
43.43.84.95
Metro: Porte Doree

Kidding Around with John Muir Publications

We are making the world more accessible for young travelers. In your hand you have one of several John Muir Publications guides written and designed especially for kids. We will be *Kidding Around* other cities also. Send us your thoughts, corrections, and suggestions. We also publish other books about travel and other subjects. Let us know if you would like one of our catalogs. All the titles below are 64 pages and $9.95, except for *Kidding Around the National Parks of the Southwest*, which is 108 pages and $12.95.

TITLES NOW
AVAILABLE IN THE
SERIES
Kidding Around Atlanta
Kidding Around Boston
Kidding Around Chicago
Kidding Around the Hawaiian Islands
Kidding Around London
Kidding Around Los Angeles
Kidding Around the National Parks of the Southwest
Kidding Around New York City
Kidding Around Paris
Kidding Around Philadelphia
Kidding Around San Francisco
Kidding Around Santa Fe
Kidding Around Seattle
Kidding Around Washington, D.C.

Ordering Information
Your books will be sent to you via UPS (for U.S. destinations). UPS will not deliver to a P.O. Box; please give us a street address. Include $2.75 for the first item ordered and $.50 for each additional item to cover shipping and handling costs. For airmail within the U.S., enclose $4.00. All foreign orders will be shipped surface rate; please enclose $3.00 for the first item and $1.00 for each additional item. Please inquire about foreign airmail rates.

Method of Payment
Your order may be paid by check, money order, or credit card. We cannot be responsible for cash sent through the mail. All payments must be made in U.S. dollars drawn on a U.S. bank. Canadian postal money orders in U.S. dollars are acceptable. For VISA, MasterCard, or American Express orders, include your card number, expiration date, and your signature, or call (800) 888-7504. Books ordered on American Express cards can be shipped only to the billing address of the cardholder. Sorry, no C.O.D.'s. Residents of sunny New Mexico, add 5.875% tax to the total.

Address all orders and inquiries to:
John Muir Publications
P.O. Box 613
Santa Fe, NM 87504
(505) 982-4078
(800) 888-7504